D0586418

Purple Ronnie's
Little Guide to
Boyfriends

First published 1999 by Boxtree
an imprint of Macmillan Publishers Ltd
25 Eccleston Place London SW1W 9NF
Basingstoke and Oxford

www.macmillan.co.uk

Associated companies throughout the world

ISBN 0 7522 1727 5

9 8 7 6 5 4

A CIP catalogue record for this book is
available from the British Library

Text by Giles Andreae
Illustrations by Janet Cronin
Printed and bound in Hong Kong

a poem for a

Boyfriend

You're a hunky handsome
heart-throb
You're a fab and groovy
dude
You're a juicy lump of
gorgeousness
A scrumptious plate of food

You're a hot and horny
lover
And if I had my way
I would smother you
in chocolate
And feast on you all day

Warning:-

As soon as your boyfriend knows you love him...

...he will start picking his nose in front of you and farting out loud

a poem about

Letting Off

Some people get lots of
pleasure
From books or from music
or art
But you seem to think it's
fantastic
To just have a really
good fart

Saying I Love You

Boys usually only say
I Love You
When they want to
Do It with you

a poem about

↓

Trousers

Men just don't know how
      to turn women on
Though they try to excite
      and arouse us
They should be romantic
      and caring and kind
But instead they just
      tear off their trousers

The Bathroom

Boys make unbelieveable smells when they go to the lav

They always leave the seat up

And they <u>never</u> clean the bath

a poem about being

Smelly

You take off your shirt

And your armpits are
whiffy

You take off your socks

And your feet are all
niffy

You give me a hug
And you're terribly
                smelly
Then you ask me to kiss
                    you
- NOT ON YOUR NELLIE!

Cuddling

Most boyfriends do not understand the point of cuddling...

...it is best to explain it to them gently

a poem about

Cuddling

I sometimes have
feelings

You don't understand

That make me confused

and befuddled

So don't go to sleep
When you turn out the
light
Cos sometimes I like
to be cuddled

squeeeze

← us having
a lovely
cuddle

Other Girls

Never trust a boyfriend who says he doesn't fancy other girls...

...he's fibbing

...blah blah
the blonde one
blah blah
blah
little
black
book
I wonder
what I'll
have for tea
yawn

a poem about

Man's Talk

Men think they can
impress us
By saying they've broken
girls' hearts
If only they'd think with
their brains
Instead of their private parts

Special Tip for Girls

Boyfriends _really_ _do_ think tarty undies are smashing

... even if your girlfriends don't

a poem about
Sex Maniacs

They dream about sex every
hour of the day
They dream when they work
And they dream when they
play
They dream about sex in the
bath and in bed
They never get naughty
thoughts out of their head

Special Tip

Boyfriends can never get tired of being told how amazing they are

you're so wonderfully lovely and smashing
what was that last bit again?

a poem for
↓
A Boyfriend

There's something I think
I should tell you
I hope you don't get a
big head
You're not only gorgeously
handsome and cool
But you're totally brilliant
in bed

Warning:-

As soon as men start drinking there is only one thing on their minds

a poem about
Men

Men think they're amazing

But I'll tell you what I
               think

Their brains are in their
                willies

And they only fart and
            drink

Sport

Boyfriends waste at least half of their lives watching sport

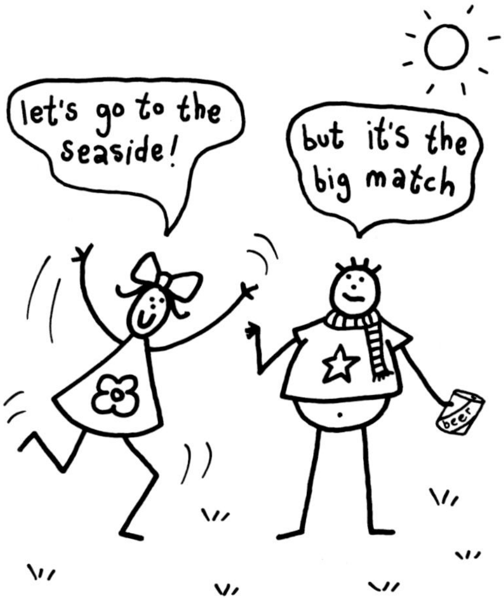
let's go to the seaside!
but it's the big match
beer

Men always like to
think they're right

2. Forget your birthday

a poem about a
Perfect Man

Most girls want a man who
is perfect
But maybe not many exist
Who've got charm and panache
Several sackloads of cash
And a willy the size of your
wrist

a poem about a
Football Fan

Why do men talk about
football

When most of them don't
even play?

They chant and they cheer

And swig loads of beer

And just watch it on telly
all day

Sneaky Tip

If you want to do something with your boyfriend - make him think it was his idea